Becoming a Trust Based Supervisor

Daniel Hansen

DEDICATION

For my mother and father and all the other's that have made me the person
I am today.

-

CONTENTS

FOREWORD

I am going to start out by telling you the answer to most of the questions I ask today, and that is simply "It depends." I know some of you will not like that answer, and some of you will want a specific guideline for every situation, but that is not what I am here to give you. There are too many situations you will find yourself in during your time in management for me to give you a set answer. Instead I can give you a framework. You can use that framework to find the answers for yourself.

Being a manager is about finding balance. There are people we consider "hard-asses" and "pushovers." A good manager is neither and both. It is about knowing when to let something pass, and when you have to get out your stick. Knowing when to listen. When to speak. When to act. And when to just stand there and let the employee talk.

Daniel Hansen

Chapter 1
"Why is he so mean to me?"
The Price of Supervisory Status

You know that other supervisor of equal level that you hate because he "doesn't respect you" or "treats you poorly." That supervisor is usually me. I pride myself in treating others with respect. I have such high standards for my staff, I see little reason other supervisors should not live up to them. This is coupled with a belief that if you are a supervisor you should be able to earn respect and suffer the consequences when you do not. I never go out of my way to be mean to someone else. But when a supervisor does something stupid (something I would have gently chided an employee for) I feel no need to sugar coat my response. I am always polite but they need to do the job their company has hired them for. They need to either fulfill their job requirements, be a decent supervisor, or they need to move along and find another job. It is my place to serve my employees and my company and suffering fools in positions of authority does neither.

I am the manager who will help train you to the best of your ability for the first few months. I will seem like the nicest guy. I will ensure you have had your training and are ready to take on your position. After that I will constantly hold up my ruler and if you are found wanting I will hold you accountable. I am the manager who has been quoted as saying, "You run a multi-million dollar operation like a kiddy park." I am the manager who once said, "If you speak to my security officers like that again you will answer your own noise complaints for a month." I was the cage manager who said, "If you as a supervisor cannot get the paperwork right you will have the amount deducted from your check. I do not even care that it would only take me 5 minutes to find the shortage." I would never dress you down in front of frontline employees. I will make sure you know that you did not meet my standards. I am the manager who will demand you respect his department and his employees. My employees deserve the best of everything. They are my family and they do not deserve poor management.

I am a firm believer that an infraction will result in a verbal or informal discipline for a frontline employees. The same infraction should mean a write-up for a lead, and a suspension for a supervisor. If I have my way the infraction will mean termination for a director. The farther you go up a ladder the easier it should be to be shoved back down. Once you accept a position of leadership, you are stating to the employees, I am an example. I am getting paid to be the example. If I mess up I will suffer the consequences. When a supervisor breaches the policies and procedures it is always a blatant breach. They are paid to enforce the rules. They do not have the luxury of claiming ignorance or simple mistake. They must be the standard. If they cannot be the standard they need to find a new line of work.

If a supervisor cannot face the consequences of not having

integrity then they need to find a new job. They are being paid a higher wage then their employees because they are expected to meet this standard. I find no reason to sugar coat my distain for a supervisor who cannot meet their burden but refuses to sit it down. There is no shame not being good at supervising. Not everyone is good at every job. But realize the job is not for you and find a better fit.

I have never kept my positions of authority because the other supervisors/directors liked me. I have kept them because my employees loved me and both my departments and I got results. We had the highest standards. We had the fewest complaints. We could handle the toughest jobs with the least amount of fuss. I may have not been liked by other supervisors, but I was respected. I may not have been the first asked to go to the party. I was first thought of when a department was in need of saving or a task looked impossible but necessary. People of a supervisory level or higher need tough love. They need standards and the company cannot afford them to fail.

My suggestion to any organization is to immediately remove any supervisors who do not meet the company's standards. The company should start this process as soon as it is obvious they will never be able to overcome their own lack in personal standards or basic supervisor skills. They are compensated for being held to this higher standard and one bad supervisor can kill a property. They will kill it fast.

Keep a "manager/supervisor policy and procedure" and make sure they sign it. Document everything supervisors do and remove problem children as soon as possible while rewarding the good ones. The company can afford to "fix" poor performing frontline employees. It does not have the same luxury toward its supervisors. This book is filled with examples of how individual supervisors can single handily destroy an organization's morale. The purpose of this book is to help you as a supervisor avoid many pitfalls. The goal is to create standards for yourself. But do not be surprised when you find yourself applying them to other coworkers.

What does any of this have to do with trust and being a trust based manager? Simple your integrity as a supervisor is your most important asset. If you lack in personal integrity you will never gain the trust of your staff. You must not only have high standards for them, but for yourself,. Often as a supervisor you will be the only one holding yourself to that bar, but your employees will see how high up you hold it. I have faith in you. I have faith in your ability to be the best.

Chapter 2
"How to Cross the River"
Completing Goals/Problem Solving

The first thing a new supervisor must learn is to problem

solve and accomplish goals. Sounds easy. After practice it will be.

The question of how to solve problems has been around a long

time though. That history is well worth looking into. In ancient

China it was common for people to test wise men to see just how

wise they were. Their answers were often used to teach others

how to live their lives. One such test was given to three sages.

The question was how to find the best way to cross a raging river.

The first Sage said that only through discipline and ordered

movement could one safely cross the river. He believed that one

should learn each rock on the river bed and each current in the river. They could then use this knowledge to create a strict plan of how to cross. Think not only of the first step but of every step you would take within the river. The dangers of the river could only be avoided by adhering to this rigid plan.

The second Sage said that one must take each step at a time. One would be weighing and measuring as one went. Test the waters and allow the body and mind to find the best path through the river's current for that moment. Think only of the first step. Only when it is completed and you know it is correct do you take the second step. Only by this testing and feeling of the water one step at a time could one really cross the river in safety.

The third Sage looked at the other men and shook his head. He said the best way to cross a river was to dive in and hope the rocks and rapids didn't kill you before the current carried you across.

So the question becomes which Sage was correct?

The answer of course is: "It depends." You will use a little bit of each sage to accomplish any one goal. That said most projects lend themselves to one form over another. Learning which form of problem solving/goal accomplishment is best for each situation usually makes itself apparent when the challenge first appears. Getting a better understanding of each form allows for a better determination of which to use. Sometimes "perfect is good enough." Other times "good enough is perfect." Remember that as in everything dealing with management, you are in a dynamic environment and a balanced approach is best.

There are projects that must be planned completely and perfectly before they should be started. All the paperwork should be filed. All the steps should be mapped. Everyone involved should be informed of each step that will be taken. These projects require exact measurement. Complete adherence to the plan once it has begun. This plan requires long periods of

preparation. It does not lend itself to quick choices. Because

there can be no last minute changes everything should be

considered ahead of time. Create one large goal, and multiple

smaller goals (steps to the big picture). Only when every duck is

in a row do you begin.

There are projects that are too fluid for such a strict plan.

Either they have too many variables, too many unknowns, or

anticipate unforeseeable obstacles popping up. These projects

should be taken one step at a time. Upon the completion of each

small step gauge your progress and how close you are to the

desired end result. As each step is completed your footing

becomes firmer and you have a better understanding of the

multiple variables involved. Those obstacles that were once

hidden reveal themselves and they can be easily avoided without

having to start completely over with your plan. This form of goal

accomplishment allows for fluidity.

And of course there are projects that can only be

completed by "flying by the seat of your pants." This may seem a rather flippant form of goal accomplishment. We must all face the realization that many times customers or employees need an answer now and will not wait 30 minutes for you to consider all sides. In the ever changing world, well let's just say it is used more than one might think or want. Either the need for immediate action or the lack of any real data (usually a combination of both) can create the need to "jump in and hope the rocks don't kill you." This form allows you to problem solve quickly. It does not lend itself to exact measurements. I once heard a Marine use the quote he heard from a drill instructor, 70% today is better than a 100% too late. This is a good summation of this methodology.

Balancing these three methods is extremely important. It is good to research and gather as much information as possible. But, at some point everything just has to go into play. It is also good to act. That said acting without thinking results in mistakes that can become costly. Knowing when to research and when to act is a key part of management, It is something that is developed

over time. In each job, each business, and each situation this cut

off point changes. You must learn how to gauge the proper

balance between researching to the point of inactivity and

completely unthinkingly blundering through a problem. It is

hoped that in order to reach management level one has

developed internal tools to gauge this balance. If not it is

something that will come with time and the mentoring of older

managers. Whether balancing is old hat or newly learned, it is

something that must become second nature. Deciding which

method of problem solving to use should be done quickly.

Firing the Arrow: A Short Story

A great story a mentor once told me about goal management is that of firing the arrow. When you are hunting out in the woods and you see a deer far off you fire an arrow. You stop. You look. You aim. You fire. Once you have fired that arrow you need to go find it. Now some people are driven. They walk straight to the arrow no matter what is in between them and it. Others get sidetracked along the way. They see a bird or a rabbit and chase after it. Only later returning to the trail to find their arrow. This story is great as it highlights that first we start where we fire that arrow. We do not necessarily start where we want to. We start where we are now. Second, it really helps to shape the idea that there is more than one path. How you follow that path is up to you. Your dedication to staying on it really impacts your ability to reach your goals, and the time it will take.

Daniel Hansen

Chapter 3
"The Queens of Drama"
Dispute Resolution

Management is often faced with multiple situations where dispute resolution becomes necessary. There are several methods and theories on how to best resolve any dispute. The two I will concentrate on are mediation and arbitration as they represent the two extremes. The tools used in mediation and other forms of what the legal field term "alternative dispute resolution" are easily applicable in the business world. Understanding the how's and why's of each form makes it easy to decide which to utilize and what role you as a manager are going to need to play. In management you will usually play the part of either an arbitrator or a mediator when an employee or customer

comes to you. It is vital to know which part you are playing as

each has separate responsibilities, tools, and limitations. Once

again as we discuss these methods of dispute resolution it is

important to look at them with an eye on balancing the two and

learning which to utilize (or what mixture of the two) for each

unique situation.

An important side note. All methods of dispute resolution

must begin with listening to each side of the dispute. No form of

dispute resolution should begin with, "Jack told me what you did,

and you are in deep trouble." All forms should also end with

some kind of decision that everyone understands. Even if that

decision is "let's wait and see." The important thing is that

everyone involved understands what has been decided (not

agrees, but understands). It is your job to ensure that everyone

will act according to that decision.

In law school we often discussed the use of alternative dispute

resolution instead of trial. For those of you who are not a part of the legal community, these are probably your primary forms of

dispute resolution. In business and life there is just no time for a

long drawn out trial. Asking someone you respect to decide, or

working out a compromise is usually the way to go. Mediation is

pretty much a fancy way of saying, working out a compromise.

That simplifies it. It simplifies it well. As a manager, you will find

yourself as one of the disputers, as a mediator, or as a witness of

some kind. Your job as the mediator is of primary importance in

this section. I will focus on it. First let us look at what exactly

mediation is.

Daniel Hansen

A. "Who gets the Orange?" Mediation:

Mediation: when there is a dispute between two or more parties and they set down with a guide. The talk it out until some kind of resolution can be arrived at. The best example I have found of why mediation is important is the story of the two young girls and the orange.

Once a young woman named Sally went into the store to buy an orange. There was only one left. She only needed one orange so this would have been perfect except for another young woman named Janet. Janet was also standing in front of the store needing a single orange. The two women began to argue over who should get the orange. Because of the loud commotion the store's owner came over to see what was wrong. He looked at the two women fighting and asked what all the fuss was about. They each claimed a greater need for the orange then the other, and again began to argue. The owner (a wise and kindly judge) cut the orange in half and said that each of them could buy half of the orange. The question is, was this the best solution? Well Sally got mad and started to berate the store owner. You see she need the entire orange peel for cookies she was making for her new boyfriend. Janet got mad and started to berate the owner. She needed a whole orange's pulp in order to finish a cake she was making her mother. Both women had no need for a half of orange. After berating the poor man, they left disgruntled.

How could this have been handled differently or better? The answer of course is it could have been handled through mediation. Instead of the owner acting as a judge, he could have acted as a mediator. As a mediator he would not have acted in any way beyond getting the two women to discuss their individual needs. He would have solicited information. Encouraged them to talk about the problem. Hopefully everyone would have discovered that they each needed separate parts of the orange.

The importance of mediation is that the mediator is a guide

not a judge. He or she is only involved to solicit information and promote discussion between people who would probably not have talked otherwise. It really just boils down to keeping the two people talking and sharing information until a compromise can be reached. The business world utilizes differing forms of mediation on a daily basis. Unlike other industries a business needs to continue to function socially to survive. They continue relationships with both internal and external partners. Whether the partner is a customer, an employee, or a distributor every dispute needs handled with an eye on continued business. Mediation helps eliminate bad blood. It forces people to come to a compromise on their own terms rather than being told what comprise will be forced on them. The mediator is not a judge. She is able to give ownership to those involved in the dispute.

This position as guide is one of the hardest parts of being a good mediator. Realizing that your opinion and what you think is the best solution is all for naught. You are not there to "make a call." You are there to get those involved in the dispute to come up with their own solution. Though this is one of the hardest

parts, it is easily the best thing you will learn in management and

will get you far.

It has been amazing to me during my time as a manager how

many problems can be solved with simple mediation. I have been

faced with two employees who seem to hate each other. I have

had other supervisors telling me the fighting will not end until one

of them is written up or fired. And a simple session of setting

them down and talking cleared the air. I say simple, but let us

face the truth. It is far from simple. It is often uncomfortably

argumentative. It is just plain painful until you get towards the

end. But the employees have ownership, and once it's done you

often have a much cleaner healing then after a judgment.

Of course the employees see it as a onetime meeting with

results. But the supervisor knows that the one meeting is simply

the point that the employees meet and greet to air their

differences. The follow up done by the supervisory staff is what

will really decide how well the mediation sticks. The supervisor must keep the two employees on the "same side" of issues. Give them shared tasks that they can agree on. Keep them away from each other on tasks that they cannot. Informal "check ins" used to gauge how each employee is doing. Look for telltale signs of the bad behavior returning. Remember that an informal check-in is not a meeting or a "set down." It is merely one person shooting the bull with another. Start out asking about their day, their week, their family, or their hobbies. If they have complaints about the other person brewing trust me, they will bring them up.

Mediation is a skill that one must learn. The rewards are less write-ups and better personnel problem solving.

Learning to listen to every side without forming an opinion helps even if you are expected to make a judgment call. Too many supervisors decide who is right and wrong before even half the information is in front of them. They get a gut reaction based on what someone complaining is saying and then go on a rampage. All without requesting other sides of the issue or finding out exactly what happened.

This kind of behavior makes the manager seem like an ass if the first story is correct. Or a buffoon when the first story is wrong. Of course being in management you will look like both an ass and a buffoon on several occasion. I can assure you it is not necessarily a negative thing to cut back on the amount of times. No matter what your company's policy is always document everything for your own files.

B. "Because Momma said so!" Arbitration:

I explain arbitration second because most managers go here by default. They really need less of an explanation of what it is. They usually only need a lesson on how to do it correctly.

Arbitration is when a person or committee is used to "judge" a specific set of facts or resolve a specific dispute. Arbitration in the business world is slightly different then in the legal field. As dispute resolution goes it is perfectly reasonable to utilize the same terminology.

As stated traditionally managers assume the place of arbitrator almost by default. They are so used to employees and customers wanting an answer and wanting it now that it almost becomes in grained to judge a situation once enough facts are in. It reflects the mentality of our current business culture which treats managers like parents and employees like children.

Everyone expects Mom to have the answer and have it now. A good Mother not only knows best. She makes sure her children listen to her.

The hardest part about being an arbitrator is that the final decisions rest with you. You are faced with a string of facts. Many times multiple sets of conflicting "facts." You are required to wring out the truth and then make a judgment that will have lasting effects on how your business operates, employee morale, and possibly your own position. The wrong judgment can leave many managers in the lurch. They can have negative impacts across the business in a variety of ways. In order to limit these mistakes it is necessary to gather facts from both sides of the dispute and, when possible, third parties.

I once had an employee come to me with a story of how not to arbitrate. The employee was what we called a "lead." A lead was a baseline employee who was responsible for those employees in their department on their shift. It seems a different "lead" (we will call her Lead B) had approached a manager telling them that two employees were complaining that Lead A was sending them home early for no reason every night. This was something Lead B had merely been told through the grapevine. The manager checked their time and discovered that yes they were going home early every night. He then approached Lead A and began berating him about these employees needing hours and needing to stay at work. When the lead attempted to explain that this was not what was occurring the manager suspended him without listening to a single word.

Upon later investigation it was found that these two employees had been asking to go home early whenever it was slow. One of them had a new born at home he wanted to get home to. The other was taking care of his ailing father. Hoping to cut back on his man hours, and please the employees Lead A was letting them go home early. Because of the manager's reaction the lead stopped letting people go home early. Man hours went up without increased need. Both employees ended up quitting in order to find work that was more sensitive to the needs of their families. Major drama ensued between those who supported

Lead A and Lead B. Their shifts became even more split then they

already had been. Lead A blamed the other for being, "a liar

trying to get me in trouble."

The manager involved could have avoided making the wrong

choice by simply asking both leads their sides. Asking the involved

employees what was going on. Instead he overreacted and

caused major drama amongst the department and harm to the

company. He completely refused to apologize to anyone

involved. The whole thing spiraled into a bigger and bigger mess.

That is until everyone involved could be brought together and

forced to face their problems. Four years later there were still

moments of drama between shifts and lowered morale caused by

this single mistake.

Many of you will recognize the manager's mistake but how

many of you will make it? I am willing to bet that in the initial

stages of your supervisory career all of you will. Remember that

fact when you are preparing to judge this manager for his major misstep. You will all make his mistake to one degree or another.

The biggest problem here was his refusal to apologize, admit his

mistake, and learn from it. Your best response to any mistake you

make is to acknowledge it, learn from it, and move on. I cannot

stress enough, never be so proud as to not apologize to your staff.

If they are to trust you, they must know that you will admit when

you are wrong and fix it.

So what have we learned here? Mainly that it is important as

a judge to gather enough information available in order to make

your choice. You have a company and a group of employees or

customers relying on you to make the correct choice. Deciding

based on what one party tells you is one of the worst injustices

you can do to anyone. No matter how good the employee talking

is, or how bad the employee they are talking about is dig deeper.

You owe it to all involved to get every side. Only then decide how

to respond.

The second thing you need to learn is that you must make that

decision. You are a manager. You are being paid to manage.

When a dispute is brought to your attention you must resolve it. If you do not you are not a good manager. Employees and customers rely on you to decide these things for them. If you do not the business will eventually come to a standstill or the drama will sky rocket as morale drops into the basement. You must get all the facts, and you must decide. There has to come a time when you shit or get off the pot. Period. End of story. Resolve it. If the manager in the above story had done nothing you would have seen lasting consequences stem from his lack of action. What the situation needed was him to respond to the complaint, but respond mindfully.

A lack of response is a response. Employees see it that way. Customers see it that way. I have seen managers who refused to assist employees in their disputes. They refused to answer questions. Those employees were even more offended then if the manager had responded in someone else's favor. All they wanted was an answer. Why some managers react this way I have never been able to discern. First, I thought it was laziness. Then, I thought it was a lack of respect for the employees. Finally, I thought it was a fear of making the wrong choice. I think, after years of seeing it, that it is a mixture of all three and more. Most managers who ignore disputes in this way show other forms of disrespect to employees. They show other signs of laziness. And many times they show signs of not really being qualified or properly trained in their current position. I do not know if this is coincidence or what, but I have never in my years seen a manager who displayed this behavior that did not also at some point attempt to retaliate against employees for perceived slights. Why these two behaviors are linked I do not know. I do know that both are detrimental to proper management and all forms of dispute resolution.

If you are one of these managers make immediate steps to change your behavior. If you have managers working for you who reveal this trait, coach them. If that doesn't work, get rid of them. If you have co-managers that show signs of this flaw, know that you are going to have to work extra hard to protect your employees from this morale killer.

Your decision will impact lives. Your lack of decision will impact lives. You are paid as a supervisor to make that call and try to make it correctly. I have faith that those of you reading this will learn without mistakes being too costly. I had heard of a story while in Oklahoma about a school official that had moments to decide which schools to evacuate with limited resources. He was told that a few newer schools with tornado proofing were out of the path of the tornado and some older schools were directly in the line of fire. He evacuated the older schools. The tornado swerved and leveled one of the newer not evacuated schools. I do not know if this story is true or false. Hearing it stuck with me. I knew then that I never wanted to enter into a job where my decisions could endanger children. When I do make a mistake it makes it easier to acknowledge it and learn from it knowing that I did not cost lives.

Arbitration is the most common form of dispute resolution used by managers in today's "let's baby-sit" management world.

It is what most employees and customers expect and even want from the managers they deal with. They want someone to come in and listen to their side, then make a judgment on what should be done. They want someone to take on the responsibility if everything goes to crap. They want direction in order to do their job. As a manager you need to learn the proper way to use arbitration and the multiple ways you can gather information. More important is to learn how your current company allows for resolution. What paperwork needs filled out. Learn any other steps needing taken. Contacting HR or your own supervisor should help clarify these steps. No matter what your company's policy always document everything for your own files.

Daniel Hansen

Chapter 4
"Who Serves Who"
Servant Leadership

An important question for any job you start is "why am I here." The first part of every supervisor's answer should be something like, "I am here to protect and serve my employees, allowing for them to do their jobs with as few obstacles as possible." Sadly too many supervisors answer with "I am here to make sure my employees work and do what I say." It is a view of supervision that has lasted for generations. It has caused continually shrinking morale whenever someone manages with this method. Servant leadership on the other hand increases morale. It helps the supervisor become part of the employees' support system. It fosters an environment of understanding and camaraderie. It engenders a corporate "family" instead of a "team." Being part of a team is good. Being part of a family is better.

It takes time and company money to train an employee to a level of competence that makes them valuable. A supervisor, who drives away a good trained employee, has cost the company a great deal of time and money. I once worked for a casino when it was just starting out. The supervisor who was head of our maintenance department was known to be a real jerk. He ignored his employees. Belittled them. He drove them away. In the first 6 months a 30 person department went through 124 people. He complained constantly that "good help was hard to find." He also complained that he had to constantly train new people.

My boss on the other hand, complained that the casino was constantly dirty. Neither of them connected the fact that this one bad supervisor drove away everyone by the time they were trained. The poor quality of our maintenance staff. When this man changed areas, the entire casino went through an overhaul.

A man replaced him who was kind to his employees. He stood up for them to upper management. The staff began sticking around. And guess what, the casino was clean. That one supervisor drove the behavior of the entire department. In so doing damaged the casino in ways that took months to fix. Not to mention lost revenue from folks that got tired of playing beside full ashtrays and dirty floors.

In the old view, the boss becomes the angry father or nagging mother who is constantly yelling at the kids to do something. He or she is a task master. The employees may pretend to work when he or she comes around, It is only a cover. The boss cares little for the employees and sees them as interchangeable. He or she refuses to enter into their personal lives. He or she thinks that the job of a supervisor is to keep people working no matter what. Nobody likes that boss.

That boss reminds me of something my mother told me once about policemen. She was a police officer for a hundred years. Hard to do when she is forever 25 years old. Through her experience she met a wide range of policemen. She told me once that cops who are doing their job, and just want to keep us safe are the best cops. But "sadly there are a lot of assholes out there that go to the academy because holding a gun makes them feel important." They like to boss people around. They like the feeling of "being in charge." These guys wear their uniforms off duty because of how "comfortable" it makes them feel.

Supervisors come from the same mold as those two types of police. The people doing their job and serving their employees are the supervisors you want. They engender Servant Leadership. The assholes who just want to tell people what to do need to go. A good way to find out which your fellow supervisors are is to ask them. If they go on about keeping people working it, or use words that indicate their disrespect or lowered view of their employees it is a red flag. You then have a strong indicator that you have an asshole who thinks his or her tie makes them a better person then those working the frontline.

If you are lucky enough to be hiring new supervisors a

good way to tell is to have them train with the employees that will

be under them. My technique was to have new supervisors work

in every department that was under me. This was whether they

would be over the departments or not. The ones that jumped

right in and served coffee and helped mop always turned out to

be keepers. The ones that scoffed at graveyard or cried around

about how "menial" jobs were beneath them always seemed to

fade away and find somewhere else to work.

Another good indication is to pool the employees

themselves. Meaning that if all of your bad employees want out

from under someone and all your good employees want to work

for them you probably have a keeper. Vice Versa the same, if

your good employees start quitting or changing departments it is

your duty to ask why. Start really looking hard at that supervisor.

Ok so we know we don't want to be that asshole. We

don't want our supervisors to be that asshole. What should we be

doing? The answer comes from my grandma who beat into me

daily that in the old days before the coming of Europeans a

woman did not look for a man with the most money, biggest home, or the nicest stuff. They did not just want a good hunter. They wanted a good hunter that gave the meat he had to the elderly and widows. They wanted the man who humbly asked others what they thought. A husband that showed respect and thoughtfulness to the answers given. The man who taught children and cared for those in need. This was the man women wanted back then. Because in that culture that man was the richest of all. His perceived wealth came from a cultural notion that in order to lead you must serve. Someone acting as leader is serving the group. Their rendition is a bit more sexiest perhaps than a modern retelling, but the idea is solid for leaders of both genders.

The group did not serve the leader. They benefited from having him or her in that position. The leader's job was to remove the obstacles from other people's path so they could live better lives and do what they needed to do. If a leader served poorly, the group found another. If one leader was a great hunter but knew little about fishing... well another person would be found to lead in fishing season. A person now says I am proud to be me. I am proud of what I have done and who I am. A person then said, I am proud of my family. Proud of my friends. I am proud to serve these wonderful people.

I have heard many different theories under the title "servant leadership" and all of them seem valuable and a step in the correct direction. My own stems from this cultural view I was raised with. It is my job to act as the grease for my employees. They have a job to do. They know how to do it. My place is to make sure to limit the obstacles in their path. They need more cups, I get them more cups. They need a clear outline of how their job should be done. I help create Policy and Procedure. They need a more efficient system of counting money. I fight to get them that system. They have a customer yelling at them. I step in and focus that customer's anger on myself. They have another employee or supervisor harassing them I step in and stop it.

I once knew a supervisor who had no respect for her employees. She constantly talked down to them. I am not sure she meant to, but she did. She was well educated and from off the reservation. The majority of her employees were from the reservation and lacked even a basic High School Diploma in some cases. She spoke to them like children. She "dumbed down" everything she said in a very apparent way. She refused to take her employee's advice on anything. She made sure that everything was "her way." She never once used the phrases 'thank you' or 'sorry' in a friendly or sincere way, at least not to my recollection.

For some reason every one of her employees turned out to be a "crappy employee." Departments dropped in morale just at the mention of her taking over. She was highly efficient and very intelligent. Yet her departments always seemed to fall apart in months of her taking over. She was a pro at numbers and 'getting the job done.' She never had a single employee willing to help her or buy into her goals for the department. She always complained that nobody liked her. Her frequent refrain was 'it's because I'm not from around here." She never once bothered to ask herself if it was actually because of how she treated her people. In her mind she treated them just fine. I mean wasn't she willing to dumb down what she said. Speak at their level? What she never considered was that they considered her condescending and rude. Even if they would not have understood her "big words" they did understand something she never could. It was her view of them as lesser.

A quick side note in response to the question, "what about the crappy employee who doesn't show up, is lazy, and/or kills morale? Can't I be mean to them? Surely I need to be the 'big boss' with them?" One can look at this question in two main ways and still be thinking in terms of servant leadership. First, your goal is to serve the other employees as well. This particular employee is becoming an obstacle to their good works. Removing him or her will be a service to the other employees. The second method is to think of what obstacle is holding this employee back? The answer is themselves and their work ethic or attitude. You are dealing with them in an attempt to help them do a better job. You do this by writing goals for them to meet. You give them the chance to improve, and the tools to improve.

The important steps here are to make sure:

1. *The employee knows the standards they have to meet.*

2. *They know the duties of their job.*

3. *They know what they cannot do.*

4. *They are informed of their poor behavior and given a chance to improve.*

5. *They are told how to improve.*

6. *They are given the tools needed to accomplish 1-5.*

7. *Everything is documented.*

That said, there is not an employee out there that should receive a poor review or get written up without expecting it. My employees know that if they fail to do their job a reprimand is coming. They expect it. At times they will even remind me to get it done. It is important to go over the standards you will use for all things. It is important to go over policy and get them use to the idea what will happen if they cross the line. If they do they decided to accept the punishment. If they do better than expected they will always receive a reward. If you fail them, then the work environment becomes one of laxity and they feel no need to try hard or do their best. Keep a policy and procedure. Making sure everyone understands it is vital. All of this is so you serve in the best interests of your employees.

A good way to keep the role of discipline and rewards in the fore front of your mind is rather simple. Before (or if it was a case in need of immediate attention after) the disciplinary action is taken set down and make a list. Write out three things you like about the employee's work. Two things you do not. And lastly the result you want out of the action. Doing this will help you to overcome your likes and dislikes, avoid favoritism, and purposely targeting an employee because you do not like them. Anytime you can think about a disciplinary action first make sure you are not being too extreme or too soft. Focus not on the person but on the behavior you want to change and how this will change it.

Even better once every few months meet with every employee for twenty minutes. I try for once every 30 days when I first take over a department but usually drop down to twice to four times a year after running it for a while. Talk to them. Nothing formal. Just getting to know them.

Always ask the simple question, "What can I do to make your job easier?" Always bring up the areas they need work. Bring up how you can help them work on it. This way when something reaches the point of disciplinary action or a wage based review comes up they understand. There are no surprises for anyone. If the employee is surprised by a bad review, you have failed with that employee as a supervisor. Make sure you also bring up good points. All the things they do well. Do not be afraid to be their cheerleader.

A leader understands their place as a servant to those who work for her or him. It is a symbiotic relationship. Like a family. A parent's job is to help the child. To foster growth and support

efforts to grow. If you tell your son to do the dishes, you do not

then stand behind him and stare at him as he tries to do the

dishes. You do not follow up by yelling about how dirty the dishes

still are when he is done. A good parent takes their daughter to

the sink. They show her how to properly clean the dishes. The

order in which to wash them. The difference in cleaning cups

versus plates. The good parent teaches the child. They teach

each step and reward them for doing such a good job. If the

daughter makes a mistake the parent will help her to not make

future mistakes. They talk to her about the mistake she made and

how to improve. A good parent understands that the child wants

to do what's right. They act as a teacher not as a tyrant.

I use metaphors like parent-child but it is important to

realize employees are adults. They are people with histories and

goals. Most of your employees will know their job better then

you do. A beverage server knows how to make coffee, clean their

area, and get their customers drinks in a way you never will unless you have worked the job for the same years they have. They do

this every day. They do it day in and day out. Your job is not to

stand in their way and try to intimidate them. Your job is to give

the tools and room they need to properly do their job.

When you manage supervisors things like Chain of

Command become important. You should not be dealing with

their baseline employees unless they come to you for help. That

is their job, their place, their duties. Your job is to assist them. To

guide them on how to supervise their people. It is not to run their

department for them. It is hard sometimes to trust in others, but

you must. I will discuss "letting go" more in Chapter 5

"Delegation," but it is important to note that when you designate

a job it no longer is yours to do. It is theirs. You need to help

them in doing it to the best of their ability. Sometimes by getting

out of their way.

If your view of supervisors is as task masters, then maybe

you should look to another job. A supervisor must be a servant to

their employees. Servant leadership fosters a feeling of family orientated corporations that can build morale. They increase the company's ability to maximize its employees. Your goal as a supervisor should be to discover what your employees need to do the best job they can, and then supply them with that.

Daniel Hansen

Chapter 5
"But I can do it better"
Delegation:
Learning to Let Go

Many first time supervisors have a problem with micro-managing their people. It is important to understand that a supervisor should only be doing the employee's job in extreme circumstances. The employee does this task every day. Probably several times a day. They do not need the supervisor's help in getting the task done. They surely do not need someone standing over their shoulder telling them how to do it "right." There comes a point where the supervisor has to let go and trust that the employees will get the job done. This is especially hard when managing other supervisors. Here the temptation is of skipping the chain of command and telling an employee's employee what to do. As in all things there must be a balance between guiding and mentoring your people while at the same time letting the employees stand on their own two feet.

Too many supervisors lean toward overworking themselves while stepping on their employee's toes. There is a fear of an employee's mistakes reflecting poorly on the supervisor. This mixed with a belief that "I can do it better" help drive this destructive behavior. One should remember to take a step back and say, "The most important tasks I do today, I must do through my employees. I must thank them for all they do."

I do not mean that if the employee is slammed and you can assist you should not. Of course you should. A good supervisor is more than willing to jump in and get their hands dirty alongside their staff. But at the end of the day everyone has their tasks. Yours is to ensure they have the tools and space to their job right. They receive the rewards they want once they have completed it.

The goal is to help your employees feel respected and trusted. Stepping in to do their job for them for no reason has the opposite effect. It is a sure morale killer. It makes the employee feel like their supervisor does not respect the job they are doing. Before you take over for an employee put yourself in the employee's shoes. How would you feel if your boss stepped in and started doing your job? You would feel unnecessary. Not respected. As if your supervisor had little or no faith in the job you do. These kinds of issues are not always readily apparent. Many first time supervisors overlook how they are negatively affecting their employees.

An example:

I once promoted a person in a technical position into the supervisor of his particular department. Despite being a great tech and being a supervisor with great potential, his department's morale started to drop. On top of this he always seemed overworked. I was at a loss to figure out why. Until I came in to watch him work.

Being a supervisor of a technical

department it was important for him to keep his

skills up. Important at times to work alongside his

people. But what I saw when I would come in was

simple. He would be working and one or two of his

employees would be standing behind him. Or he

would be standing behind his employees telling

them how to do each little thing. It was

detrimental to the department.

His employees felt like they were useless.

They asked themselves why they bothered coming

in at all. They felt belittled because he would take

over or "walk them through" every simple

problem. They felt like they knew their jobs. They

did not need a constant watch dog. He on the

other hand, felt like it was his responsibility to

make sure everything was done and done

correctly. He was working himself to death trying to complete the department's frontline technical tasks and his supervisor tasks.

Honestly the worse experience I have had with this was a mistake I made myself. Framing part of my own management style off of my immediate supervisor when I should have known better. It was my first experience at managing other supervisors. I went from managing around 3 departments and about 40 employees including a few team leads to managing over 200 employees including 9 supervisors who had leads under them. My manager had always felt free to go directly to my employees and inform them of what he wanted to see and how he wanted things done. I never thought much of it as we usually discussed the situations beforehand. There were problems though of employees going directly to him with problems. He made choices for my departments that I would never have made.

When I stepped into my position, I was allowed to choose much of my supervisory team. I picked the best. It is still probably one of the best teams I have worked with in my years in

management. They knew their jobs. They knew their employees.

They cared about the property. They were constantly surprising

me with great ideas for positive change. They were proactively

solving their employees' and customers' problems. For almost a

decade this group grew, changed, and even when people came

and went it remained one of the best. I was excited to be head of

such a great management team, especially when we managed

such an important and successful employee base.

We were given a mix of departments that covered the

gamut from great workers to drama queens. It is not every group

that has a real family atmosphere from the baseline employee to

the director. With these supervisors it was not long before we

took some of the most drama filled departments and helped them

become families that worked productively to ensure the

property's success.

But in the midst of all this success I started to notice a few

of the supervisors taking a hard look at changing areas and pulling back from doing their best. I could not understand why these top quality supervisors were making some poor choices, or failing to make choices that seemed apparent to me.

One night as I gave my delegation speech to a first time supervisor (yes over the years I have developed patented speeches in order to train employees and supervisors or handle reoccurring issues) it hit me why these supervisors were reacting as they were. It is easy to see a supervisor take over on writing a memo. To see them working on a technical project. It is less apparent when that supervisor breaks the chain of command.

I was skipping my supervisors on key issues involving their departments. I was going straight to their leads, and even worse to their employees and assigning tasks as I saw fit. It was like a lightning bolt struck me. I realized that I had been doing their job. It was their responsibility to make sure that their departments got these tasks done. I had chosen the best team because they could get the job done. Instead of trusting in them to do what I had hired them to do, I disrespected their abilities and did it all myself.

I had to learn the hard way that being a supervisor is in this regard like raising children. You tell them what you can. You teach them what you know. At some point you have to let go and hope they make you proud.

Well it should go without saying that I immediately stepped back and reevaluated how I used the chain of command. Ironically I had pushed and pushed for the strictest chain of command I could in the hopes of avoiding what had happened to me with my previous manager. Yet here I was doing exactly what he had done. Jumping the steps. Hurting my employees' morale. It was hard. Probably one of the hardest things I have ever learned in management. I began to tell the supervisors what I needed from their people. I let them choose who would do the tasks and when they would get done. I held them accountable. I created a constant dialogue as I worked through them. It was, as I have said, their job to discipline and work with their own employees, not mine. As the director I was responsible in making sure they did their jobs, and did them correctly, but it was not my place to do their job for them. Let me repeat this statement as it is vital. It is the supervisor's job to make sure the work gets done and done correctly. It is not the supervisor's job to do the employee's work for them. The best way of course is to empower your employees. Give them the tools they need and get out of their way.

It is ironic that most supervisors are constantly telling their employees, "stop worrying about other people, worry about yourself and your job." But the supervisors so often fail to take their own advice. So let me give some advice; they were hired to do their job, you were hired to do yours. Now let them do their job, and you concentrate on your own. Your job is to oversee. To watch for patterns and to reward or correct behavior. Yes your employees will make mistakes that need fixing. Learn to mentor them, and not take over for them. One makes them feel supported, the other makes them feel unnecessary.

Daniel Hansen

Chapter 6
"It's not my Fault"
Fix Instead of Blame

One of my biggest pet peeves is when someone claims, "It is not my fault." Mainly because at the time of major problems I care so little about whose fault it is. I want to know how to fix the problem. I want to know how to make sure the problem never arises again. Once the problem is fixed and everything is running smooth there will be plenty of time to discover who or what was at fault and fix that as well.

My view is coupled with the idea that an employee's failure is the supervisor's failure. If the supervisor had been doing their job correctly the employee would not have failed. Hence it be funds the supervisor to fix problems rather than trace the blame she should know leads back to her anyway. So the best approach is to assume you are to blame and find out how to fix the problem.

In business as in life it is the child who tells their mommy; "that's not my fault." "I didn't do it." Or the classic "Timmy did it." When supervisors, like parents, approach their children they do so wanting to correct behavior and problems. They do not want to listen to a litany of why it is someone else's fault. Why the employee is not to blame. Why the so sad world of everyone is making that person the scape-goat.

One must realize that employees who react this way to having problems brought to their attention usually do so out of fear. They have a history of punishment for doing something wrong. Usually they have worked mostly under supervisors who yell or discipline for wrong doing. Supervisors who have failed to understand that it is the actions/mistakes that are bad not the employee.

These employees internalize their actions and behavior. They say things like, "that is just who I am, your yelling at me for who I am." But how a person stacks cups or shows up late is not "who they are." It is a learned behavior that they can easily fix. Concentrate not only yourself but the employees under you on fixing the problem instead of assigning blame. Help them by concentrating on their bad behaviors and attitudes rather than on them as people. In this the business world agrees with Gandhi when he said, "hate the actions not the person."

The job of a supervisor is to fix problems not assign blame. If there is an employee's actions to blame the supervisor should of course mentor the employee. Discipline the person as needed to insure that the problem does not occur again. An employee that accepts the blame and helps find a solution goes a long way in redeeming the problem in my eyes. An employee that accepts there is a problem and tries to find a solution without worrying about blame goes even farther.

An employee who says things like, "there is a problem with

x and it is Joe's fault," needs to be retrained. Someone in a supervisor position should lose that position until they can become reeducated. The proper thing to say is, "there is a problem with x and this is the solution." If the problem stems from a single employee it can still be worded in this way. For example, "There is a problem with how Joe stacks his cups. His lead needs to let him know how to properly stack the cups. The lead will have to change her training routine to make sure that new and old employees know how to stack their cups."

Notice that I did not blame Joe, nor did I blame the lead. It would have been easy to say, "It is the lead's fault, why the hell did she not train Joe on stacking his cups." But that goes right back to finding blame. Who cares. What we see is a problem with a two prong solution;

P: *Joe does not know how to stack those cups,*

S1: *Retrain Joe on how to stack the cups,*

S2: *Have the lead change how she trains and keeps up on that training.*

Taking this approach not only fixes the current problem but goes a long way in making sure that the problem does not occur again. If instead the supervisor just suspended Joe there would be a band aid fix. The one to five days Joe was off the cups would get stacked right.

An example from my experience:

A beverage department was constantly having problems with waste. They constantly had to throw away cups, straws, creamers, and lids due to overstocking. The graveyard lead (my employee) made note of the amount of items his shift found in the trash when they came on. The culprit was of course untrained employees trying to do better jobs by overstocking their self-serve stations. When my boss brought it up to the swing lead, she flipped out. She told him it was the dayshift lead's fault. The graveyard lead's fault. It

was two or three employees' fault. So he, for once,

went on an investigation of the problem. His

investigation was all about whose fault it was. He

spent weeks trying to pinpoint exactly what

employees were overstocking. He never bothered

to go out and look himself of course. He worked

solely through the swing lead and her supervisor.

By the end of the month, they had a

detailed list of which employees were at fault.

None of the supervisor's or lead's favorites of

course. Yet the overstocking was still a problem.

The trash can was still full of unused product. So

they worked hard to increase the names on their

list and pinpoint even further who kept causing all

of these problems. And yet no matter what names

they added to their list, the trash kept piling up.

Finally, the graveyard lead asked me what

to do. We sat all of our employees down and explained to them the problem. When dayshift got there we sat down with their employees and their lead and explained the problem. That night we did the same with the swing shift. I went one step further and posted in each of the coffee shops the problem. I requested that they not overstock. I asked that they discuss with their lead or fellow employees how to stock properly. We purposely did not treat it as a disciplinary problem. We instead treated it as a training problem. The note basically implied that, 'hey we know some of you were not trained properly here is how you fix it."

The swing lead flipped. She spent over an hour with her boss cornered complaining that we had overstepped our bounds talking to "her employees." Her supervisor shrugged her shoulders and agreed that I was out of line. My boss berated me that cornering the employees was not the way "we solved problems." The culprits "needed punished" and we were helping them avoid it. And yet the trash cans started to empty. The overstocking started to stop. Ironically only the swing shift failed in completely fixing the problem. But my boss had been specific. I was not to mess with the shift, and so I waited.

One night several swing shift employees stayed over to help graveyard, due to call in's and it being busy. Two of them asked my graveyard lead how to properly stock their self-serve. He was taken back because these were long time employees, not rookies. But he showed them. They thanked him. Two nights later we had several swing employees ask if they could stay over. As the month wore on more and more found reasons to "stay late and help out."

What we found was that the employees on that shift were so scared of being disciplined for overstocking they never asked how to stock properly. Their lead had not taught them. Yet now that they faced discipline if they came forward and admitted they had not known. They just hid how they did it from their lead. Once they realized that the graveyard lead and I were willing to train them without "ratting" them out, they all found reasons to stay late and "help" us.

When the time came for my boss and the swing supervisor to discipline the 'trouble makers' only two names were on the list. Both what I consider 'favorites' of the swing lead and supervisor. So the whole thing was dropped. My boss even had the gall to tell me that he had handled it how I wanted. By yelling at all the employees and posting a memo that "anyone caught doing it wrong would face termination."

Servant Leadership is perhaps the crux of my problem with people assigning blame. It is the supervisor's job to mentor and help employees. When an employee does something wrong, the supervisor should step in and help them to do it right. If the employee continues to do the job poorly, then discipline may become an option. Even then discipline should have as its goal performance/conduct correction, not punishment.

One is not seeking to punish but instead to correct behavior. When discipline will not correct behavior, termination should be the obvious choice. If an employee will never change, there is no reason to discipline other than to show the needed history. The problem will not be fixed while keeping the employee. The job of the supervisor is to fix problems.

Sometimes a supervisor is faced with an employee of this kind. The most important advice I can give is to create a paper trail. The last thing a supervisor wants is HR sending the termination papers back due to lack of a history of problems.

Finding a problem should always be followed by find a solution. It does not have to be "the solution" but merely a solution. The all American phrase everyone knows is, "that works." Do not waste time and energy finding out who is to blame. Use that energy and that time to fix the problem. Your business will thank you. Your departments will run much smoother. Your company has spent time and money training the employee. Why waste all that time and money because you failed to train them well. Correct the problem and if needed take the time to retrain the employee/deal with the behavior problems.

Remember that the more time you spend trying to find out who to blame is more time your customers go without your product. That employee and you should be out with the customers, selling or manufacturing whatever it is you do. Every minute you spend fixing blame is time lost with your customers and employees. When the CEO comes and says, "I received a complaint about this problem, what are you doing about it?" It is the child that says, "Oh that's Joe's fault." The first thing a good supervisor says is, "I am aware of the problem. I have taken steps to correct it."

Chapter 7
"Nobody else does it."
Leadership:
Diversification and Integrity;
Your Life as an Example

It is amazing to me how many new (and old) supervisors

fall into the two traps of lacking personal standards and holding to

personal prejudices. Targeting employees they dislike. Favoring

employees they like. Failing to hold themselves personally

accountable to basic standards in both their personal and

professional lives. These two areas seem to be connected in that

they stem from the same problems. Either a lack of integrity

and/or a failing to understand their place as supervisors. We will

need to look at these problems. Look at examples of these

problems. Then discuss ways to cure ourselves of the many

symptoms that they engender. If you have read Chapter 8 it's

techniques will help overcome some of the problems with

favoring and prejudging employees. This section will concentrate

more on why you should overcome the problems.

What does lacking of personal standards have to do with

diversification of the work place? The question seems an honest

one, and I hope my answer is clear. A person with standards

holds themselves and their employees to those standards. When

they hire and promote they base those choices off of the "best

employee." Not the best white employee, or the best related

employee, or even who they like the most. In my time as a

supervisor I have hired and promoted gang bangers,

homosexuals, ex-convicts, hippies, republicans, Muslims,

Christians, people of all races and genders, and even at least one

Wiccan that I know of. These people meet my standards for

supervisors and employees. I could not deny them a chance

based on my views of their lifestyle. The work force under me

became extremely diverse mainly because I paid more attention to my standards then my personnel prejudices. I never had to go out and seek diversity because the society in which I live was already diverse. All I had to do is drop my blinders and rely on my basic standards.

So let's take a look at what exactly standards are. An example of personal standards can be found in something as simple as dress code. Most supervisors either do not have an official dress code, or nobody is around who can call them on that dress code. I have heard several new supervisors complain to me, "but so and so wears short skirts/polo's, why should I wear a suit." I usually let them vent for a bit. Then I look at them with that 'stop being a baby' look all supervisors and mothers learn at some point. And then I start in on them about personal standards. It is not about what other supervisors are wearing. It is not about what their boss is wearing. It is about what they feel they **should** be wearing. It is important to step back and realize, my dress reflects my standards.

I can choose to hold myself to a high standard and wear a suit. I can choose to throw my standards out the window and wear something less appropriate. One needs to ask themselves, what would I want my employees to wear if I was my own boss. Would I be proud of my employees if they dressed this way? The basic thing you are looking for is your own standard for yourself and your job. What example are you setting to people if you wear a skirt that barely drops below your waist? Is it an example you want your employees to follow? Dress Code is just an example. But it is a good one. It is such a visible one. An employee that sees you will mimic you be mindful of the example you set.

Do not get me wrong I am not discussing how you dress on Friday night. I am talking about how you dress on Monday morning. You should be free to be whoever you want away from your workplace. But you represent your business while on the job. That is not to say all of business will want you in a suit. It is to say you should be paying attention to what they do want. If you are taking a job where everyone in that position dresses in

drag consider that before accepting the job.

I once had a supervisor who was young enough to still be

in the "cool crowd" at work. As I walked the floor I overheard an

employee use the word "shit" in front of this supervisor. The

supervisor just stood there and listened to the whole story. He

never said a word. I walked over and pulled the supervisor aside.

I am sure he thought I was crazy, because of how intense I

got over this simple slip by an employee, but I drove home that it

was not the employee's slip I was upset over. I was upset with

the supervisor's. An employee who respected his supervisor, and

knew that supervisor had standards would have never uttered

that word where customers could hear. I knew he was a WWII

buff. Mainly from Video Games, butt had sprouted into a real

interest in the era. He was also a strong Christian. I asked him if

he had ever read of a man named Camus. He had not so I told

him this story from Camus (a story I have not read since college so

bear with me):

Camus lived in France during the Nazi occupation. He was not what you would call a supporter of the Occupation. And so he was picked up by a group of soldiers who put him in the back of truck so they could haul him away. He was not arrested because of anything he had done. He was just on the wrong street, on the wrong night, looking the wrong way. In the back of the truck there were 12 other men and a Catholic Priest.

The Priest was there to "watch over" the prisoners in the interest of legitimizing the Nazi's pulling them from their beds at night. Basically he had been pulled from his church and put in a truck. He sat in the truck all night. He got to go home in the morning still alive if he behaved.

The soldiers argued. It seems they had a quota. They had not yet filled it. So they took it upon themselves to grab 2 more people. One was a boy around the age of 12. The boy sat at the

back of the truck near the gate. Across from him

was the other lucky winner of a Nazi Truck ride.

Besides the boy was Camus, and across from

Camus was the Priest. The truck hit a bump, the

boy fell out. He just laid there in the road. Three

people noticed; the other man, Camus, and the

Priest. All they had to do was keep quiet and the

boy would avoid the camps. The soldiers had not

bothered to get his name. They would never

bother looking for him. It was the Priest that yelled

for the soldiers to stop and go get the boy.

I asked the supervisor if that Priest had done the right

thing. The answer was no, he should have kept quiet and saved

the life of one of his flock. The Priest took on a responsibility by

becoming a priest. He chose to take a position in society where it

is not ok for him to act like the "normal guy." A supervisor may not be doing something as important as saving 12 year old boys from the Nazis, but she still has a duty.

She has a duty to act when she sees something wrong. She has accepted a job to not "be part of the crowd." When someone does something wrong, it is her job to say something. If she fails the employees who see it will assume that the actions were ok. A supervisor must be a supervisor. They must be seen as a supervisor. They must act like a supervisor. When an employee does badly, the supervisor should not wait for another employee to speak up. She should have already spoken.

You are the supervisor. Part of your job is to be an example to everyone. This should include your off duty time as well as your on duty time. Many supervisors feel that how they act off the job is of no consequence to their on duty performance. This is simply not the case. Your employees are both smarter and more judgmental then you will ever give them credit. You think they are your drinking buddy. Think again. They will be telling their coworkers of all the things they saw or heard that you did. A lack of integrity or professionalism outside of work has a direct effect on how your employees and coworkers perceive you and treat you at work. If they know you are out sleeping around their respect will drop. As it drops they will listen less and feel freer to ignore your authority.

I once had a supervisor work for me who liked to drink. Really liked to drink. He would take his department out almost every night and have a roaring good time getting drunk and being the center of attention. The employees loved him. He was everybody's best friend. But when it came time to discipline his employees or ask them to do the simplest tasks they laughed him off. They thought he was a great drinking buddy. They could not see him as their boss. How can anyone see the Bar Clown as their supervisor? How can anyone respect him/her?

I have seen another supervisor who spent her money on the craziest and stupidest things. She would get her children hired in departments they had no business being in. Then allow them to talk to her in the most disrespectful ways. She was always broke. She was always on a rollercoaster ride of emotions.

She was never respected. She would even go so far as to ask her

employees and other people's employees for "loans." She was a

morale killer. Nobody knew what kind of mood she would be in.

Everyone was afraid she would be pressuring them for a handout.

Afraid of what kind of reaction they would get if they turned her

down. She was unstable. Because of this she destabilized her

departments, and bred disrespect everywhere she went.

Employees judge you. If you do not measure up, getting

them to do what they need to do will be harder than ever. They

will laugh you off. Simply ignore you or worse yet refuse to

accept your authority. The first time an employee tells you, "You

can't tell me what to do," or they ask, "Why should I listen to

you." That will be the time you should realize this employee does

not respect you.

Before you go on and on about what a horrible employee

you have stop and take a look at the perception of yourself you

have given to that employee. Stop and look to yourself. If you have put off the wrong impression that employee has no reason to respect you. Trying to force respect will end in multiple confrontations or the employee undermining your authority. Neither of these results is acceptable. The best way to avoid them is to be someone the employee can respect.

I want you to notice what I said there. Your first step should be to look at yourself not the employee. This does not mean you do not sanction the employee for their behavior, you should. But it is important to realize that a supervisor is more than a personal individual. They are a title and a position. That position requires someone to fill it. It includes duties and responsibilities that you must fulfill. If that means cutting back on drinking or changing the areas in which you drink then so be it. If that means changing how you dress, or modifying your behavior then so be it. Most supervisors are well compensated for fulfilling the roles they are given. You must live up to that role. You must look at the goal of your job. You must set your own standards for reaching that goal.

Your goals should include integrity, perception, standards, and a work ethic. You should set down and define your job's role and place in the corporation. You should also write out and define what you think a person with integrity is. What perception you want to give to those in your life. The standards you have. What kind of job you should be doing based on you work ethic. I usually add my answer to a simple question: "why am I here?" The answers to these questions will act as a guide as you move forward.

It is good to make broad statements but do not allow your statements to only be broad. Get specific. What I mean to say is, it is easy to write, "I am here to make sure my guests receive traditional tribal hospitality." This may be a good start, but sub list this with things like:

"My guests will be offered free drinks in five minutes."

"I will do my best to provide for my guest's comfort as if they were in my own home (both through my employees and through my own actions)."

"I will listen fully to anything my guests have to say."

"I will respond with respect to everyone even when it is difficult to offer that respect."

"A manger does not have a romantic relationship with his/her employees."

"A manager has X as an attribute."

These kinds of lists help guide you as you move forward, and act as a reminder. When your employee asks you to take a trip to the bar for a weekend of binge drinking and strip club hopping, your list will force you to ask, "Is this perception what I want to give to my employees."

The discussion on integrity could go on and on with examples of how people speak. What they say. How they act. How they treat others. What they are willing to "not see." And who they choose to associate with. But it really boils down to being a supervisor is a balance. You should seem friendly and part of the group. You should also be impeachable. A person to be respected. Should you go drinking with your employees? The answer is as always "it depends."

Your job might need a strict authoritarian. In which case no. Your job maybe in need of someone with a more "friendly" touch. Most of this will depend on your employees and the environment of your corporation and community. Perhaps you do have a few drinks and socialize. Letting your employees get to know you as you develop personal relationships. But it also probably means that those few drinks should not turn into a drunken-puking-fest of debauchery. Your goal should be to keep your employees respect, while following your own standards and keeping your own integrity.

Chapter 8
"I know he hears me, he just doesn't listen"
Personality Tests; Communication with and Motivation of Employees

There are a host of motivational tools and personality tests on the market. Most all of them are beneficial for first time supervisors. The important things to remember are that employees are people. Each one different. None of them fitting nicely into a generalized box, but those boxes used in these books are definitely helpful in dealing with your people. These tests usually break people up into four main categories. These categories are created by graphing where a person lands based their traits along two main axis. The first axis is between

Introverted and Extroverted, and the second between Feelings Based and Rules Based.

Finding out if someone is introverted or extroverted is as simple as finding out if they prefer dealing with people or not. Do they get energy from groups or from silence. Ask them what the term "down time" means to them. How out going they are, how shy? An introverted person is usually shy and uncomfortable with attention. They may or may not like large groups. Even if they do, they usually want to be part of the crowd. Not the center of the party. They many times prefer to work alone, or hidden within a group. They rarely take leadership roles. It forces them to stand at the forefront of the group. They can make good leaders, and often want a leadership role. They just have a harder time coming to grips with the leader's need to stand up and be seen.

An extrovert is just the opposite. They want to be the center of attention. If they work alone it is so that there is not a group to take their credit. If they are in a group they want to be heard and seen. The extrovert is the class clown or the class president. They need attention and bask in it. They often seek out leadership roles in order to insure themselves the attention they seek. The can make great leaders. They often have to be reined in as they learn that at times the supervisor needs to allow her employees to make the big splash.

In extreme circumstances the extrovert is the girl dancing alone on a table. The introvert is the one quietly in the corner sipping her drink. Few people are those extremes. Most of us fall somewhere in the middle. Usually we can still be found on one side or the other. Not just the person's personality but the circumstances can change this as well. The guy, who is an extrovert at the bar, can become introverted in a classroom or vice versa. We all know the guy who just will not shut up in class. He is constantly needing to be the center of attention, who then turns into a mute table hugger if asked into a dance club.

Finding out if someone is a rules based or feelings based personality is as easy as asking them a few simple questions. A rules based person will more often quote a rule, or come from a very "logical" or legal point of view. It is hard for them to understand why people feel the need to discuss their home life at work. They will shy away from conversations that are too "emotional" and will appear wooden or uncomfortable when personal questions and concerns come up. The rules based person is much more comfortable in a structured group with detailed policies and procedures. They want guidelines, and they want them followed.

Their personality often seems rigid or too strict when they are extremists. They make no exceptions and often become too inflexible in extreme circumstances. They often become leaders in order to install order. When they are good supervisors they see their job as enforcers of Policy and Procedure and seek equal treatment for everyone including themselves. The best quality that comes from a rules based approach is that it is equal to everyone. Here is the rule, follow it. They are the supervisor who holds their standards above all else, and are often let down by the rest of the supervisors who take a more feelings based approach.

A feelings based person is much more comfortable in talking about how they feel, and how others feel. They are emotionally driven and see the world in a much less black and white way. They are comfortable making exceptions to the rules. It is the people that are important not the rule. Feelings based people are much more likely to internalize disciplinary action both in accepting it and giving it. They have a tendency to feel that discipline was an attack on their person or that they must do it because the employee 'let them down.'

Feelings based personalities can make good leaders, because they are flexible in how they react to rules. Adapting rules to best fit the circumstances. They tend to be seen as to wishy washy to someone who is rules based. Their desire to create exceptions are seen as playing favorites or being soft. In extreme circumstances they are seen as chaotic. They follow their heart through a problem. The employee that faces bereavement in their personnel life could ask for no better or understanding supervisor though. They tend to argue emotions based theories rather than logic. Putting an emphasis on their own gut reaction in certain circumstances.

I have often tried to come up with a better way to word "rules based" and "feelings based" as what the words imply are not really the distinctions wanted. Really it breaks down to what they rely on to react to situations. Rules based rely on external sources. Quoting something from outside of them and feeling safe because there is a standard to base all choices off of. Feelings based rely on internal sources. They use words like 'instinct' or 'gut reaction.' Wanting to work from the heart. Neither view makes a person more or less fair.

A rules based person will feel that when the rules are applied equally and objectively the world is a fair place. A feelings based person will feel that rules are only fair if they can be modified to fit each specific situation. Again most people tend to lean one way most of the time, but go back and forth given the circumstances. Someone may deal with their kids in a feelings based way, only to become much more rules orientated at work.

The four types then are:

A. *Introverted-Rules Based*

In my experience accountants, auditors, vault tellers, Surveillance, and IT folks are usually in this category. They are people who want as many facts about a situation as possible, with few opinions. They excel at those simple yet boring tasks so many others dread. Put them in a small room with lots of information and they will never let you down. Put them in the chaos of a Casino Floor needing snap decisions and they will probably fail.

They usually avoid conflict, which means they are not very good at it. They tend to either be passive aggressive, becoming explosive when pushed to far or given too much interpersonal stress. Given a list of numbers and facts they can often shock everyone else with an immediate spotting of a mistake or finding a pattern. I have known vault tellers that could glance through a stack of papers and tell you exactly where the mistakes were made.

B. *Extroverted-Rules Based*

These people should be cops, security officers, chefs, or anytime you want rules enforced equally. Someone not afraid to get involved. They are usually good at taking a project from start to finish. They may get bogged down if there is too much gray area. As a supervisor this person will be strict. They may be disliked by others who are not rules based. They have standards and they will tell you how to meet those standards and woe to anyone who fails to live up to them or do them wrong.

They appear (usually because they are) as rigid and uncompromising. Suspending an employee for missing days, and who cares that their kid was sick. But their departments always have well written policy and procedures and their employees always know when punishment is coming. There is not a lot of surprise in dealing with this kind of person. You know what they want, you know how they want it, and you know the reaction when it is not done their way.

C. *Introverted-Feelings Based*

These are good HR folks, councilors, ombudsman, or anyone who needs to listen. They do not seek to be the center of attention. They usually make really good listeners. Though often caught in their own interpersonal drama, they are usually willing to listen to yours. They are empathetic and understanding of problems not their own. They are often easily discouraged and made cynical due to dealings with rules based folks. They at times feel unimportant when surrounded by extroverts.

In my experience I have the most difficulty dealing with this group. They seem overly sensitive and often clam up at the slightest perceived insult. They often just want someone to listen to their problems. But rarely speak up until they reach a boiling point. They at times feel slighted due to the fact that they listen to everyone else and damn it nobody asks how their day went. They of course are unlikely to respond if you ask them how their day went, but that is not the issue. You should have asked.

D. *Extroverted-Feelings Based*

Chaos is how I heard one personality test explain this type. They are the center of the party, going with the flow. They are the center of their own world. They make sure they are the center of yours. They will be mostly unproductive in an enclosed arena, or one with no audience. If given a task that requires them to work alone (such as writing policy and procedures or a book on management training) and they will wander away. They will be looking for an audience, getting little if anything, done. Great on a busy casino floor where chaos rains and snap choices need made. They are extroverted enough to walk amongst the customers and employees and talk to them all.

They are usually well liked. Though seen with some trepidation by introverts. Their ability to adapt to new situations makes them flexible enough to work in an environment that is in constant flux depending on the customers and employees present. Often needing reigned in if professionalism is going to be upheld. This can be difficult as it is often just too entertaining to watch them for you to react.

Being an extrovert, it always seems to me that both introverted groups let things build inside until they finally explode over a problem. Going from "it's ok, I'm fine" to inconsolably pissed like a light switch. Then holding a grudge for long periods of time afterwards. Extroverts tend to argue passionately getting heated quickly, but setting it aside and having a beer together just as quickly. One of my best friends is most assuredly a rules based extrovert, and we use to argue so viciously that people thought we were sworn enemies. We always followed up with a laughing discussion on how her kids were doing. Like everything these categories are limited in their use. Everyone has a little bit of all of them. It is still useful to see what kind of person you are talking with. It is also good to know your own biases. In end when questioning if you should use it or not the answer is, "It depends."

Daniel Hansen

ABOUT THE AUTHOR

Daniel Hansen started working in Indian Gaming in September of 1997 at a native casino, and he spent his entire adult life learning everything he could about how the industry works and actively managing staff, which he still does as a Casino Executive. He is an enrolled member of the Village of Kotzebue and a shareholder of NANA Corp. His background allows him to see Native Casinos through the eyes of a businessman, a lawyer, a philosopher, and still remember true success does not necessarily come just with a bigger bottom line, but an empowered tribal membership and an improved community. He firmly believes in Servant Leadership, and only by empowering others will he find success in this life.

Basically he is super awesome...

www.ingramcontent.com/pod-product-compliance
Lightning Source LLC
Chambersburg PA
CBHW070821180526
45168CB00002B/710